NEAT SNAKES

By the same author

Poetry

Faultlines (with Y. Christianse and N. Krouk)
The Great Wall of Instinct
In the Cage of Love's Gradings
Be Straight with Me (for teenagers)
Sensual Horizon
The Human Project: New and Selected Poems
Ground
Midday Horizon (ed. With P. Boyle and M. Bradstock)
Harbour City Poems: Sydney in Verse 1788-2008 (ed.)
Contemporary Australian Poetry (ed. with J. Beveridge,
J. Johnson and D. Musgrave)

Criticism
Microtexts

Other
Ngara: Poems, Essays and Meditations (ed. With John Muk
Muk Burke)

Neat Snakes

MARTIN LANGFORD

PUNCHER & WATTMANN

First published in 2018
Published by Puncher and Wattmann
PO Box 441
Glebe NSW 2037
http://www.puncherandwattmann.com
puncherandwattmann@bigpond.com

National Library of Australia Cataloguing-in-Publication entry:
  Langford, Martin
  Neat Snakes
  ISBN 9781925780093
  I. Title.
  A821.3

Cover design by Tim Langford
Text design by Christine Bruderlin
Printed by Lightning Source International

This project has been assisted by the Australian Government through the Australia Council, its arts funding and advisory body.

PREFACE

I developed a liking for aphorism when I read La Rochefoucauld
in my twenties – a restorative to the excesses of a young man's
imagination. Until then, I had never seen our emotional lives
portrayed with acerbity. Different cultures develop different ways
of describing behaviour, and there is a tartness to the French
observations which is not found in the work of many other
nations. It took me some time to realise that just because their
comments were sharp, they had not given up on the emotions
they were portraying. I explored other aphorists: as well as the
judicious French (La Bruyère, de Chazal), there were frantic
Austrians (Kraus), philosophical Germans (Lichtenberg),
shrewd but whimsical Spaniards (Ramón) and the humorous
Irish, English and Americans – although the English-speaking
traditions (Sydney Smith, Oscar Wilde) have often tended more
towards bon mots than aphorism: in the continuum between
entertainment-effect and truth-telling, their instinct has typically
been for the former. Many of Wilde's sayings, for instance, have
enough truth in them to spice the delivery, but not so much as to
weigh them down with refusal to compromise.

In the twentieth century, modernist experiment generated
a different short utterance: the surreal one-liners of poets such
as Ritsos or Michaux. Given that science was proceeding with its
own attack on the familiar, I became intrigued by the possibility
of combining the defamiliarisation of the poets and scientists
with the lucidity that the aphorism had traditionally employed.
Sometimes, writing can feel like an attempt to articulate an
aesthetic, and although one may only approximate it occasionally
in practice, its presence as an ideal – the search for a tension
between lucidity and strangeness, so that the phrase can never
quite settle – provided a kind of stiffening for the project, a
background pressure or test which nevertheless helped to keep it
afloat.

There *is* a problem with aphorisms: unlike poems or stories, they do not offer those sanctuaries of place, habitus or event which readers so like to dwell in – and which give writers something to flex against. As literature rather than philosophy – as attempts, that is, to capture not just the idea, but its weight as well – their brevity does not allow much time for the investments of the reader to be confronted by the circumstance the aphorism portrays. Something like this does have to occur, however, and it has to be done quickly: as so often in writing, the solution seems to depend on getting the shape right. I can only hope that, now and then, at least, I have been able to provide these sentences with enough internal tension – to give them enough shape – to compensate for their lack of the more extensive pleasures.

ML

I can imagine justice, but not love.

~

Here comes beauty, trailing its distances ...

~

Christ's fate was sealed when he said he loved everyone.

~

Our fantasy lives flow easily, being continuous with our love of power. But thought requires effort – we are still getting used to it.

~

Even *not being loved* is a construct.

~

Vigils are maintained against immodesty – by peers obsessed with celebrity.

The beautiful are not exempt from the need to be brave. But we treat them as if they are: it is how we destroy them.

~

Someone keeps taking the stage away.

~

Good looker, good tackle, good idea: all the meanings of *good* blend together – into the one stream of approval and immunity.

~

Easier to manage one's integrity if the criteria are simple.

~

Language has not changed us much.

~

Triumph is the only version of happiness cognate with narrative.

Romantic love begins in dreams of status: it can found a relationship, but not a society.

~

The elegance of the utterance will not save you.

~

Sometimes, morality is just the average of everybody's honour: the collective expediency of face.

~

In the Old Testament, to be human was to be obedient. In the New, the human was defined by compassion. And now: it is a matter of dismay, at the frailty of our ideals in the face of our biology.

~

Self-esteem is impossible without inferiors.

~

First, read for the position of the speaker.

Lives too, take on lives of their own.

~

The first rule is that one must take the game seriously.

~

The modern world excels in the variety of ways in which status is represented.

~

Hope and envy are twins.

~

The bore seeks witnesses to his servitude.

~

Before love can exist, there must be a distance that needs healing.

The aphorist trusts the reader more than the argument.

~

Celebrity culture is an economy of ego-needs, and as such is governed by the bid and counter-bid. All dreams of worth will be betrayed.

~

Choices are just words, unless they imply the possibility of a loss.

~

The heart is a sense-organ too.

~

Like a mother, the New Testament turns towards the father of the Old: *Don't be too harsh on him Jim.*

~

Our characteristic failing is our refusal to acknowledge the other, in the name of our need to shape story.

The artist betrays the person you are, out of loyalty to the person you might be.

~

The dance-steps grow kind and inventive. But the solitudes are implacable.

~

They were trying to create a society where all indebtedness could be resolved with money, and courage need never be required.

~

The great thinker can't get the spiv with the throwaway questions to show more respect.

~

Trust murmurs *compromise* and *security*.

~

The modern political dialogue is a device for the management of the envies through repetition and simplification.

It would be unbearable to find out.

~

If there are no rules, one does not become free: one succumbs to the tyranny of the genes.

~

An audience is a type of god, from whom it is possible to win approval with one's performances.

~

The joker distributes the looks.

~

The dark side of sexuality is not just an afternoon of innocence in leathers: it is the physical expression of an obsession with status and power.

~

The word and the body must search for each other in bed.

Personality is one of the mysteries.

~

We invented the afterlife because we could not imagine our non-existence.

~

The right combination of mirrors should keep you from falling.

~

In the beginning was the word — because there is no time without language.

~

Reason is beyond our control.

~

And what arrival could we believe in?

Society is an argument about a body.

~

Art gives a shape to consciousness. But not everyone is conscious, nor wishes to be.

~

The stupid have the advantage.

~

The desire to be perfect is a passion of the insulated spaces.

~

Humans are bound by a shared subscription to the values that keep them apart.

~

Love is not blind: it is all too predictable.

Sometimes, it is true, art requires the suspension of disbelief. But not as much as societies do.

~

The ego is endlessly reborn, and the word is infinitely patient.

~

How much does one owe to one's others, and how much to oneself?

~

Laughter is an eruption of discomfort at the interstices.

~

How we hate moral ambivalence: it plays such havoc with our responses.

~

Talent is just handstands and somersaults, if it does not engage with the other.

There is no art without abandonment. But nor is there art without self-consciousness.

~

There is a link between morality and pronunciation: those who wish to rein in our animal spirits must speak clearly, in order to be heard.

~

Say we made peace. How could we bear to read history?

~

The vanities of the individual are rightly condemned. But the vanities of the tribe are the myths that sustain it.

~

The natural world is liberating precisely because it is indifferent to the anxieties of the self.

~

Ineptitude aside, most bad design is an indulgence of our passion for status and power.

Integrity has a slightly bitter taste.

~

Sex, poetry and silence: the three consummations of language.

~

Human or animal: in extremis, we are one or the other.

~

In the city, people believe they are responsible for their fate. But that is an artefact of the decisions the city allows. For the Boeotians, such a claim would be hubris.

~

At the centre of the history of unhappiness is the fact that sex must be negotiated. But how could it be otherwise?

~

How could a god tell the difference between crying and laughter?

We are wary of the flesh-porn of the men: it is too reductive; it does not let the woman speak. But the selection-porn of romance – its aggregated reifications of choice – is just as reductive, and both sexes will spend their lives in its thrall.

~

Will anyone remember your story? Will your death be a linguistic event?

~

Reading is either an act of power, or of engagement: the reader is either a voyeur or a lover.

~

Don Juan understood that the dreams of the credulous weren't so innocent.

~

Together we domesticate the silence.

~

The *weigher of hearts* keeps a list of the things we have laughed at.

There are no great orations with complex theses.

~

One can, it seems, be excused from the implications of the text if the writer is flawed.

~

We have reined in the angers and lusts with a network of laws. We have sacrificed freedom for justice.

~

No-one chooses what to think: thoughts choose themselves.

~

Both the comic and the tragic are just lenses.

~

A shared prejudice is a bond. But reason is no basis for affinity – insisting, as it does, upon the right to challenge every claim.

First, the hero must contact the ethics committee.

~

We spend our lives arguing for the terms under which we will
be judged.

~

We find relief in sport precisely because it has no meaning: its
drama is expressed in numbers, and numbers contain no moral
burden.

~

If only we didn't wish to be loved uniquely.

~

How can I trust any claim that has not been weighed by the body?

~

The indebted maintain their vigil against the free.

The most difficult negotiations are between levels of understanding.

~

When the middle-aged lean close, their histories lean with them.

~

By themselves, facts cannot sing: not without the feelings that resist them.

~

The American dream, the Australian dream: their only concern with equality is for an equal chance to write oneself superior.

~

What use are the model's eyes?

~

Terrible to contemplate the way loyalties develop.

If we are not careful, the world will disappear beneath the sign.

~

Love cannot bear the presence of judgement.

~

We emerge out of nothing, but regard our disintegration
as unjust.

~

When you fight back, you become stronger, and narrower.

~

Many would rather die than love.

~

The working-class parents could hardly be admitted to the world
they had sought for their children.

We are vain about our cleverness: fashionistas of the sign, we look down our noses at the animals.

~

We seek self-destruction for the same reasons we seek power: to escape an insupportable present.

~

Our ancestors made the same gestures, but in a different play.

~

Nothing is at stake for the gods: they are amoral *because* they cannot die.

~

We resist many injustices, but not the random distribution of beauty.

~

Reconciliation is as moving as loss – but less frequent.

Teach the free man how to praise. But praise takes the indirect object: one praises something *to* someone. To whom do we offer our praises?

~

What happened to the taboo against envy?

~

All the bad things can be explained. But happiness is inexplicable.

~

We graze information as the cattle graze grass. And like them, we pause, and look up; look around and resume.

~

We still have that trust in the efficacy of reason which destroyed Oedipus.

~

And so we present our credentials – again, and again.

Desire *is* one's relationship to the earth: it is the gravity of one's narrative.

~

We domesticate the world with our art. But if the art is any good, it will not trust the idea of *home*.

~

The teenage gang is the archetype. All other patterns are refinements of this – or attempts to resist it.

~

Beauty is either a delusion or a proof.

~

There will be no end to story: it will keep plodding after us.

~

Which is more terrible – the tyranny of a Stalin, or the credulity of his mourners?

It is a truism that comedians play gangsters well. Both nurture their angers, and direct them with intent; both avoid unmediated contact with the other. But the gangster will not sacrifice the self, as the comedian does.

~

Desire ignores the weeping in its choices.

~

Wonder blossoms in rational spaces — and vanishes in hierarchical ones.

~

Banter is a way of exploring which claims will be allowed.

~

The purpose of most entertainment is to keep the present at bay.

~

We prefer those whose criteria allow our achievements to be visible.

Give me the strength to act according to my understandings.

~

Language is either a hall of mirrors, or a regression of gods.

~

Some lives are all sexual dance.

~

If you seek approval, you should do it so nobody notices.

~

Not everyone expects to be loved.

~

I do not know whether we offer the beautiful too much. But we offer the homely too little.

Which are worse, the airs of the successful, or the excuses of those who have failed?

~

If you can't tell an insight from a platitude, you will need to disallow all generalization.

~

Night after night: our appetite for vicarious triumph is inexhaustible.

~

To listen to us talk, you would think that our purpose was to seek out comparisons.

~

Art that does not gesture beyond the sign may be admirable for its skill, but it will not elicit wonder.

~

Most people are defined by their audiences.

Love must negotiate the crisis of the partner's ordinariness.

~

We cannot use language without making judgements. But judgements require us to step away in order to see – to enter the distance we peer back from, dreaming of *close*.

~

The selectivity of beauty is a failure of the imagination.

~

Achievements are hands at a rock-concert.

~

For many, any activity not driven by an anxiety is oppressive.

~

Some lives are defined by numbers, and some by words.

The lens has replaced the god as the instrument of witness.

~

Advertisements are true enough – in hell.

~

No vista is big enough which does not include the observer's non-existence.

~

The imagination can be crushed by too many artefacts.

~

The heart grows sick of talk. It would rather sing.

~

Mostly, people do not want to 'be themselves': they want to be simplified into favourable judgements, and turned into currency.

No-one realised knowledge would require so much uncertainty.

~

Most injustices originate in an inconvenience.

~

The ultimate imperialism is of superior explanations. Who can resist them?

~

The tongue that arranges the food for the teeth can make beautiful music.

~

From now on, we will only ever entertain ideas provisionally.

~

Heroes create, through their courage, an access to choices.

The purpose of art is to make the heart conscious.

~

We laugh outside the boundary, and ease ourselves back in, as the laughter dies down.

~

The journalists are reviled for telling us the lies that we pleaded for.

~

We learn to expect such modest levels of happiness.

~

There is a loneliness in beauty: as if it made one feel just a little bit naked.

~

Common understandings are grounded in common assessments of power.

Most lives clarify, over time, to a few simple themes.

~

Beauty is the subject talking.

~

Words slide – but not like desires do.

~

The comic book, the action movie, the celebrity magazine and the totalitarian government: they are all either visual artefacts, or visually expressed, and the hierarchies they assert cannot be challenged by words – they must be physically displaced.

~

A life without sensual attention is merely a narrative.

~

The worker and the billionaire both believe morality is just a teat for the middle classes.

Fetish: the absurd metonymy of the hormones.

~

Our biological natures are constants. It is the nature of the human that we keep re-inventing.

~

Knowledge made it possible for us to proceed — in such a way as to ensure we can never arrive.

~

Obsessive love is joyless. Joy requires an awareness of the other as other.

~

All spaces should respect the costs of their construction — and gesture beyond them.

~

For the artist, there is little difference between a lack of imagination, and a lack of courage.

In the capitalist dream, each of us is an arc of autograph. But who, apart from the child, believes in the tales one makes up?

~

If our society fails, it will be because the complexity of the decision-making becomes greater than our capacity to construct discourses in which the decisions can be explained.

~

Justice only matters to those who can imagine the other.

~

Vicarious triumphs are at the heart of our culture: dreams and stories of usurpation and replacement; of striding through fields of reward, sowing loss and abjection. But vicarious sex is taboo.

~

The capacity of the lens to create hierarchies based on looks is overwhelming the capacity of language to generate communities based on behaviour.

~

We would rather be invulnerable than ecstatic.

It is an impiety to try to imagine one's god. It is the one thing a god cannot bear.

~

All idealisms partake of the loneliness of the will.

~

Winning: is that the best we can do?

~

If happiness is not continuous with courage, then it is something else: escapism, indulgence; permission, relief.

~

When you enter an elsewhere, the last thing you learn is its aesthetics.

~

The picturesque was both a step towards and a step away: a gesture towards the other that put a limit on its otherness.

We operate closer to capacity than we care to admit.

~

Knowledge for its own sake: what is the point of that?

~

Cultures only forgive each other when they can write a common past.

~

Sex in a partnership is like God in society: it is the basis for everything else – and therefore must not be represented.

~

We grow impatient with naïve explanations. And with those which are beyond us.

~

Hard to accept we have no right to happiness.

We used to dislike it if an object did not honour its source: if a timber desk paid no attention to its grain, if plastic was painted like metal. Now, in a world of 'elaborate transformations', no-one knows where anything comes from, nor expects to.

~

Spin requires an established trust to manipulate. But as people learn to adjust for it, their trust is corroded: next time, they will be less likely to believe. And it is not just their trust that is undermined: it is the whole idea of a credible explanation. Spin runs the risk that all versions will be discredited; that there will be no arguments left in the public domain: just the candidates talking to themselves, and the incoherent wind-ups of the radio jocks.

~

If the development of the individual as a legal and cultural entity (Sappho, Tu Fu, Falstaff, Blackstone) derived from a blossoming of names for the self, then the sense that language is changeable and ungrounded – deriving from the many ways language has of considering itself – may be the second great emergence of self-consciousness: but of the provisional nature of meaning, this time, rather than the self.

~

Few believers can articulate their beliefs.

The credibility of the bad guys is rarely in question.

~

If you want someone to love you, you must capture their imagination.

~

In art, a frame, being conceptual, is an absolute: one has either set this material aside – for meditation free from consequence – or one has not. In life, however, the frame around a jurisdiction is a projection of power, and as such is endlessly contested.

~

It is difficult to articulate ideas in broad Australian: to do so runs counter to its economies of the mouth.

~

The decencies of the dead resonate more than their achievements.

~

We have lifestyles, not lives, said Robert Dessaix. If so, it is because our decisions do not cost enough.

The purpose of most emotion is to make itself redundant.

~

We cannot save the other. But we can offer our companionship.

~

If everything can be managed, if the chaotic and unforeseen can be expelled – then all the little emperors need never leave their childhoods.

~

Some people only exist when defined by a rival.

~

There is a special despair of the insulated spaces, of the endless layering of artefact.

~

No matter how carefully we manage our masks, some of our faces still bleed.

For many, to take one's role in a weave of narratives is enough: why should one also engage with the others that one finds there?

~

We were humans who meditated on the divine. And now we are animals who meditate on the human.

~

Happiness rarely strays far from the voices in the room.

~

No joy without courage.

~

If we are not allowed to look at it, then it is probably a source of power.

~

Reason is such a monster now: few imaginations can embrace it, and still breathe themselves.

Interiority withdraws the body from the moment like a first step towards sorrow.

~

Bores translate the world into facts to oppress us with. And then lean at us out of the loneliness of the discourse of power.

~

In the world of the artefact and the sign, all self-assertions are equally valid: there are no means by which to argue otherwise. Where decisions must be made, however, involving others or unknowns, such assertions are absurd – obsessed with the self, when the self is not at issue, and insisting that behaviour is a matter of preference – or self-expression – when necessities are at stake.

~

Our responsibilities are infinite, and impossible to prioritise. How could we manage without being obtuse?

~

Over time, all partnerships tend towards a balance of power.

Celebrities are bound by neither language nor time. They have no pasts or futures; they are not subject to rules. They exist only in the ether of exemption from limit.

~

The idea of *the campsite* does not subtend the difficult claims that *the home* does.

~

Increasingly, we measure the weight of a death by the extent to which a narrative was completed.

~

The passion for status and advantage must never be acknowledged – even to oneself: it would damage one's sense of modesty and belonging.

~

The lover knows what death is.

~

It will be sufficient, in hell, if our understandings are intact.

The man wanted to be more than an emissary from the land of seed.

~

Too many lead lives that are otherless: that are solely defined by position and goal.

~

The tabloids use the bereaved as vehicles for their own love of power.

~

You can't change your personality. All you can do is to explore its possibilities.

~

Attention to detail can dry up the sources of joy.

~

All the relationship's meanings emerge, over time.

The children of wonder are not like the hierarchs. They do not have enough anxiety about power to see things as the narrative requires.

~

A cud of vicarious triumphs, a daily mastication of satisfying endings: we can at least be saved in our entertainments.

~

How convenient: the indeterminate subject is incapable of agency – and can never be accused.

~

All foundation-myths are retrospective.

~

Contemporary political discourse is an autonomous loop – spoken by reports, and addressed to statistical likelihoods.

~

Democracy was going to free us from hierarchy. But hierarchy has subtelised, and swarmed.

The cynic never quite loses the hurt of the world's first refusal.

~

The dream of story is to transcend itself. But its fate is to remain trapped in the shape that it gives to events.

~

Art should take long views like zen, but be grounded as turnips.

~

To know is to replace the other with the sign. To understand is to leave the other room to dance.

~

Our myths used to conceive of us as eaters and begetters. But now that we define ourselves by a language-based sense of justice that originates in compassion, most tales resolve to the one failure-myth of the human.

~

I am always dismayed, when good-looking people voice opinions I dislike.

When she married, she exchanged her imagination for a house.

~

On Planet Language, anonymity is non-existence.

~

There are so many innocent pleasures for organized omnivores.

~

Opinions are rarely as distinctive as voices or gaits.

~

Our rights may be artefacts of context and power, but we claim them as if they were sacred.

~

Say we are God inventing Him- or Her-self. Then God is going to have to find a way to disarm the compulsions of status, or we shall never let go of the narrative.

It is not easy to make the transition from a life defined by survival to one in which aesthetics is possible: one must re-write the basis of one's morality.

~

The more people there are in the conversation, the more it will sound like a dispute about pecking order.

~

There is often little point in countering arguments — unless one can challenge the anxieties that underpin them.

~

The middle-aged yearn through a lattice of sensible judgements.

~

Beauty is a sensual apprehension. Even when we talk of the beauty of an equation or a sentence, we cast it in physical terms, and assess it as design: shape, balance, tension, economy, elegance.

~

The god of Thanksgiving is a god of domestic narratives. Few offer gratitude for black holes or volcanic eruptions.

Technology baffles the instinct for closure: the speed of change overwhelms those stable contexts in which a self can write a satisfying end. Nowadays, we are simply released, mid-stream, from the flux.

~

We remember the proximate dead. Everyone else just disappears into the calm beyond ganglia.

~

There are, it seems, only the two possibilities: either one's understandings are projections of one's needs, or one's life is a negotiation with one's understandings.

~

The best is only available to the attentive.

~

Love constructs a morality for two. But there is nothing moral about its beginning or end.

Awe, wonder and delight: all our other responses are expressions of interest.

~

People spend their lives gazing at celebrities. But few would wish to be one: they know how treacherous their admirers can be.

~

It is not enough to be an intellectual. How could it be? People are not exempted from responsibility by the quality of their talk.

~

At the heart of every romance, there is a doubt about identity.

~

All beauty is excessive, in the presence of death.

~

Just when we thought we were free – the archive became universal.

The journey towards the other *is* the journey towards the self.

~

There is no such thing as the human outside contexts which read for humanity.

~

To the unimaginative, all differences are absolutes.

~

The meekly selfish are easier to deal with.

~

We photograph both people and landscapes, but struggle to frame them together.

~

I am not bored by other people. But I am bored by the limited nature of our interactions.

We avoid acknowledging the acts of power our lives are built on with animus and ingenuity.

~

We love our celebrities, for their glamour, and we love to see them fail, for their presumption.

~

One cannot believe in the uncanny if nothing is heimlich.

~

The beautiful only exists on the edge of the chasm.

~

Who will we laugh at, if no-one is excluded?

~

Hell needed to be horrible. Horror upon horror upon horror. And even then, it wasn't enough.

All pleasantries are fake, in the presence of desire.

~

In the kitchen, beauty and horror are inseparable.

~

Sympathy is an ideal substitute for action.

~

What could it mean, we will one day be whole?

~

Anxious about their materialism, they gave generously at Christmas.

~

Eros and justice inhabit one flesh — but two tongues.

The arc from iconoclast to conservative is a seamless one,
anchored at every stage by the resentments of the ego. And it
remains as hard as it ever was, to imagine beyond them.

~

No-one wishes to be summoned by story.

~

To privilege feeling ahead of necessity is to invite death in.

~

The self is the centre at the margin of all other worlds.

~

No-one wishes to be accused of the exercise of power. We would
all rather be photographed, standards aloft, in the last, exalted
moment before the new state is proclaimed.

~

So the women walked out of the gaze, and into the pure world of
words, where desire could not follow.

Numbers for decisions and necessities. Words for the gestures of the human.

~

No-one should make claims about themselves: we shouldn't be so presumptuous. Yet in the modern world, that is how we live: we compile lists of claims; we turn our lives into tokens.

~

In the migratory narrative, place is not for living in – it is to let one know how far one has travelled.

~

For many, the earth can only be imagined as a habitat for humans: no other life-forms are worthy of notice.

~

Every culture has its own way of averting its eyes.

~

High fashion is a declaration one would rather be useless.

Sometimes the courage is the last thing that anyone notices.

~

Every assertion has its co-ordinates.

~

The more attentive one is the more one will have to defend the unorthodox views that attention provokes. Which is why people choose to be vague.

~

Status, triumph, exaltation: there are few things sadder than our dreams.

~

Intelligence is like courage: one must never talk about it.

~

A world without unknowns is a room without windows.

The idea of guarding against one's biases is incomprehensible to those for whom reality is a function of self-image.

~

In time, all one's rivals fall away before the ticking of one's skull.

~

Happiness begins in a sense of the self's provisionality: the self-obsessed weep when they speak.

~

The journey is an illusion of the subject-lens.

~

No specific difference is fundamental: racism, sexism, class. We will nominate any difference we can build an advantage on.

~

War will not go away if we promise not to think about it.

You will travel farther hitched to an anxiety.

~

Some conversations are just dances for the gyroscopes of self-respect.

~

One cannot accuse others of the politics of envy, without signalling one's own high self-regard.

~

The world-views of the right are projections of their anxieties about self-esteem. Challenge the world-view, and one challenges their self-respect: which is why their responses are so often irrational and disproportionate – they are protecting what cannot be argued for.

~

There are few things more useless than understanding without courage.

~

The beak is as important as the wing.

The suburbs are unfashionable because of their spaces. Who will confirm your importance – or testify that you belong?

~

We can only manage histories of wrongdoing by othering the perpetrators first – even when the crimes were committed by ancestors.

~

The generosity of the lover does not extend to freedom for the beloved.

~

Companionship is sturdier than love: it does not pretend it can save you.

~

The heimlich is apprehended at the level of the sign: an archive of the pre-digested which collapses if one pays close attention to the things one thinks one knows.

The only questions permissible in a hierarchy are those about the acceptability of one's behaviour.

~

In the ideal protocol of the gaze, the man becomes aware of the woman's beauty without lifting his eyes.

~

Bred for survival, they were told to dilate in the new world as warm, moral blooms.

~

Those with much to lose are hampered by their attachments, and do not fight like those with everything to gain.

~

Easier to ignore the insufficiency of one's own love than one's partner's.

~

Usually, we prefer the lie, because it answers a deeper need than most truths do. Not the deepest need – but for somewhere to live, for the terms we can live by.

To be considered as a partner, I must be strong enough: I must eradicate my vulnerabilities. So how could I be a good partner?

~

We do not look at the world anymore: we look at images of the world.

~

It would be terrible if the democracies did not survive, because they had looked after their citizens so well they were reluctant to defend them.

~

Multiculturalism will delegitimize all our histories.

~

The implications of our understandings grow more onerous every year. Better to refuse to understand.

~

The aestheticization of food takes us one step further again from respect for the animal.

For many, magnanimity is inconceivable: how can one act against one's interests?

~

If one's irony is more forceful than the position it undermines, it will become the new centre of gravity.

~

Did I make myself up, or did others? Am I subject or object?

~

If each age has its characteristic hubris, ours is to claim that our spaces do not derive from the exercise of power.

~

The Americans have cliff-sized statues. We have the big merino and the giant prawn. And I trust what this says about our attitude towards enlargement and abstraction.

~

How can we interact without objectification?

One can only 'construct one's identity' in a protected space: one free of the insults of a disruptive universe — in a law-abiding consumer society, for instance, where the shapes the subject takes are acts of choice, rather than the unselfconscious expressions of one's struggle to survive.

~

Nature is all utility. But human environments that are solely utilitarian repel us. We seek the aesthetic gesture: something to tell us we are more than just a function of indifferent forces.

~

Some women solve the impossibility of imagining sex by insisting it can only exist as touch.

~

Celebrity invites one to believe, when the questions grow hard.

~

When people defend a narrative, they are usually defending their role within it.

Large skies reduce the credibility of the structures on the ground.

~

Without attentiveness, a life is just a filibuster.

~

Distance turns the road into an elegy.

~

We need so much space now, to grow in: so much we can drown.

~

If romance is a dream of recognition, what do you want the mirror to reveal?

~

The spaces in which we negotiate self-interests are the real battleground: the sites in which the decencies are possible. Beyond them, self-interest wears on like the ticking of genes.

In one nightmare, justice is only permitted in public, where no-one can touch.

~

In some prisons, there is an answer on every door.

~

Our tolerance of reason varies with the threat that reason represents.

~

The ground between ugly and beautiful is a no-man's-land: it has not even qualified for a name.

~

It is our fate to be uttered as story. But I despair of a love which is only conceived in narrative terms – as status, triumph, possession; as territory, debt or exchange.

The happiness I trust is not pure, but aware of the cost of choices, and the weight of understandings. Continuous with courage, it is a sharpening that refuses the one-dimensionality of our sanctuaries. It might take the form of relief, but it is too self-aware for the theatre of self-esteem. Riddled by words, it is, nevertheless, not language; haunted by narrative, it inflects beyond story to the recognition of our others – an attentiveness which leans towards communion, but which never loses its independence.

~

The battle for the future is being fought between those who seek to justify the projection of power, and those for whom power can never be justified in the face of disrespect for the other. As always, the former own all the simple, malleable words, and most of the guns, and the latter only reason, and an impulse – call it 'loyalty to wonder' – which hardly looks like anything, if it is spelt out like that. Yet we cannot allow ourselves even to imagine that the latter will lose.

~

Mostly, our triumphs are framed as apogees of self-assertion: instincts attempting to mean, in imaginaries which do not function beyond self-interest. It is impossible to think of them without thinking also of the silence into which they will vanish. But our attempts to resist them leave a great deal of poetry in their wake.

www.ingramcontent.com/pod-product-compliance
Lightning Source LLC
Chambersburg PA
CBHW031006090426
42737CB00008B/709